8/5/08
10.95

Phonological Awareness FUN!

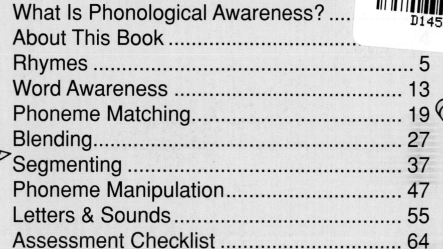

Table of Contents

D1456252

Managing Editors: Angie Kutzer, Allison E. Ward

Editor at Large: Diane Badden

Contributing Writers: Susan A. DeRiso, Ada Goren, Alison LaManna, Jan Robbins, Dayle Timmons

Copy Editors: Sylvan Allen, Karen Brewer Grossman, Karen L. Huffman, Amy Kirtley-Hill, Debbie Shoffner

Cover Artists: Nick Greenwood, Clevell Harris

Art Coordinator: Rebecca Saunders

Artists: Pam Crane, Theresa Lewis Goode, Nick Greenwood, Clevell Harris, Ivy L. Koonce, Sheila Krill, Clint Moore, Greg D. Rieves, Rebecca Saunders, Barry Slate, Donna K. Teal

Typesetters: Lynette Dickerson, Mark Rainey

President, The Mailbox Book Company™: Joseph C. Bucci

Director of Book Planning and Development: Chris Poindexter

Book Development Managers: Cayce Guiliano, Elizabeth H. Lindsay, Thad McLaurin, Susan Walker

Curriculum Director: Karen P. Shelton

Traffic Manager: Lisa K. Pitts

Librarian: Dorothy C. McKinney

Editorial and Freelance Management: Karen A. Brudnak

Editorial Training: Irving P. Crump

Editorial Assistants: Hope Rodgers, Jan E. Witcher

www.themailbox.com

©2003 by THE EDUCATION CENTER, INC.
All rights reserved.
ISBN10 #1-56234-524-9 • ISBN13 #978-156234-524-2

Fun With Phonological Awareness

Whether reciting favorite jump rope chants or creating silly tongue twisters, children love to play with language! Experimenting with rhymes and other sounds is not only entertaining, but it is also educational. In fact, activities such as these can strengthen phonological awareness—a key factor in your students' literacy development.

What Is Phonological Awareness?

Phonological awareness is the ability to think about and manipulate different parts of spoken language. It includes the understanding that sentences are made of words, words are made of syllables, and syllables are made of sounds, or phonemes.

How Is It Different From Phonemic Awareness and Phonics?

It's no surprise that *phonological awareness, phonemic awareness,* and *phonics* are easily confused terms since they all relate to sounds. But they are not the same. Phonological awareness is a broad term that includes phonemic awareness. It involves both large and small sound units. Phonemic awareness refers to only the smallest sound units, or phonemes. Children who have strong phonemic awareness can hear the individual sounds of words. They can omit sounds, add sounds, or even substitute sounds. Both phonological and phonemic awareness tasks are oral.

Phonics tasks, on the other hand, involve print. Phonics refers to letter-sound correspondences—the knowledge of how letters represent sounds. Because of its link to letter sounds, success with phonics depends on success with phonemic awareness.

Why Should You Teach Phonological Awareness?

Phonological awareness is one of the strongest predictors of reading success. Students who have strong phonological awareness have a firm foundation on which to build reading and spelling skills. Students who lack phonological awareness are likely to struggle with reading. Phonological awareness does not develop automatically, but it can be taught. And since phonological awareness is so strongly related to reading success, instructional efforts are well rewarded!

How Can You Fit Phonological Awareness Instruction Into Your Schedule?

Phonological awareness is a critical factor in reading success, but that doesn't mean it should occupy a large percentage of your instructional day. Students can make significant gains in phonological awareness with brief daily activities, sometimes only ten minutes long. Many of these activities can be woven into your regular routine, saving precious time for other types of literacy instruction.

What Are Some Important Things to Keep in Mind?

1. Students' needs and skills

Some students do not need direct instruction to acquire low levels of phonological awareness, such as rhyming. They require explicit instruction for only the more advanced levels, such as changing sounds in words. Other children need explicit instruction for all levels. Phonological awareness instruction is most beneficial for students in the early grades, but it can also be helpful to older struggling readers.

With instruction, some preschoolers and most kindergartners can achieve success with the following tasks:

- recognizing words as separate units
- rhyming
- matching sounds
- blending sounds
- breaking words into syllables

2. Levels

Within each level of phonological awareness, there are varying degrees of difficulty. It is easier for students to work with larger sound units, such as syllables, than with smaller units, such as phonemes.

Some advanced kindergartners and many students at the end of the first grade can also manipulate sounds.

3. Literature

Phonological awareness instruction is enhanced when it occurs in the context of literature. There are countless children's books and traditional rhymes that incorporate alliteration, rhymes, and other sound-related fun. Read the material to students once or twice for enjoyment before focusing on selected phonological elements.

4. Phonics

Pairing phonological awareness instruction with letters helps students transfer their newly acquired skills to reading and writing. A combination of phonological awareness and phonics instruction is more effective than either type of instruction alone.

About This Book

Phonological awareness is a prerequisite for beginning reading and helps lay the groundwork for more advanced reading. This book provides multiple ideas for facilitating this awareness, and they can be easily incorporated into your instructional day. The more than 80 phonological awareness activities allow you to choose those that match your students' needs and interests. We've also included a dozen activities that focus on letter-sound correspondence, because pairing phonological awareness instruction with letter-sound instruction is more effective than using either type of instruction alone. Using the activities in this book will help strengthen your students' skills in phonological awareness and put them on the path to reading success!

How Does This Book Reinforce Phonological Awareness?

This book is divided into six main levels of phonological awareness: *rhymes, word awareness, phoneme matching, blending, segmenting,* and *phoneme manipulation.* We've sequenced these levels from easiest to most difficult, but it is important to remember that some of the levels, such as blending and segmenting, are complementary. It may benefit your students to engage in activities from several levels during a single time frame. Also, keep in mind that within each level of phonological awareness, there are varying degrees of difficulty. By continually observing your students during the activities, you can make informed decisions about the level of difficulty that is appropriate for each of them. (Use the Assessment Checklist on page 64 to help you do this.) Finally, research has shown that instruction in phonological awareness can be made more effective by connecting this learning of sound segments to instruction with letters. So for your youngsters who are ready to move into letter-sound correspondence, use the suggested activities in the seventh section of the book.

In Every Unit

- A teacher reference page that includes
  — key background information on the featured level of phonological awareness or phonics
  — a list of highlighted skills
  — special teaching tips
- A selection of activities that focus on the featured level of phonological awareness or phonics
- Literature connections
- Handy patterns and reproducible activities to accompany some suggested activities

4

ogical Awareness Fun Phonological Abareness Fun Phonological Awareness Fun Phonological Awa
ogical Awareness Fun Phonological Awareness Fun Phonological Awareness Fun Phonological Awarenes

RHYMES

Elephants are known for their big ears, listening capabilities, and high intelligence. Have your students turn on their "elephant ears" as they complete these rhyming tasks to increase their phonological awareness.

Understanding rhyme is an initial phonological awareness skill. Students can train their ears for the sounds of words by hearing and using rhymes. In fact, early knowledge of nursery rhymes seems to be strongly aligned with the development of more abstract phonological skills as well as the development of beginning reading skills!

The activities in this section will help your students do the following:

1 improve listening skills

2 explore the rhythm and sounds of oral language

3 identify rhyming words

4 enjoy, engage in, and respond to literature with rhyming text

5 discriminate between rhyming and nonrhyming words

6 create series of rhyming words

Many opportunities to strengthen rhyming skills occur naturally throughout the day. When planning activities with rhymes, keep the following progression of skills in mind (ordered here from least difficult to most difficult).

1. **Recognize rhymes.**
   Do *cat* and *bat* rhyme?
2. **Discriminate between words that rhyme and those that don't.**
   Which word does not rhyme: *cat, bat, cap, hat?*
   Which of these pictured objects rhymes with *hat?*
3. **Supply rhyming words.**
   How many words can you name that rhyme with *cat?*

5

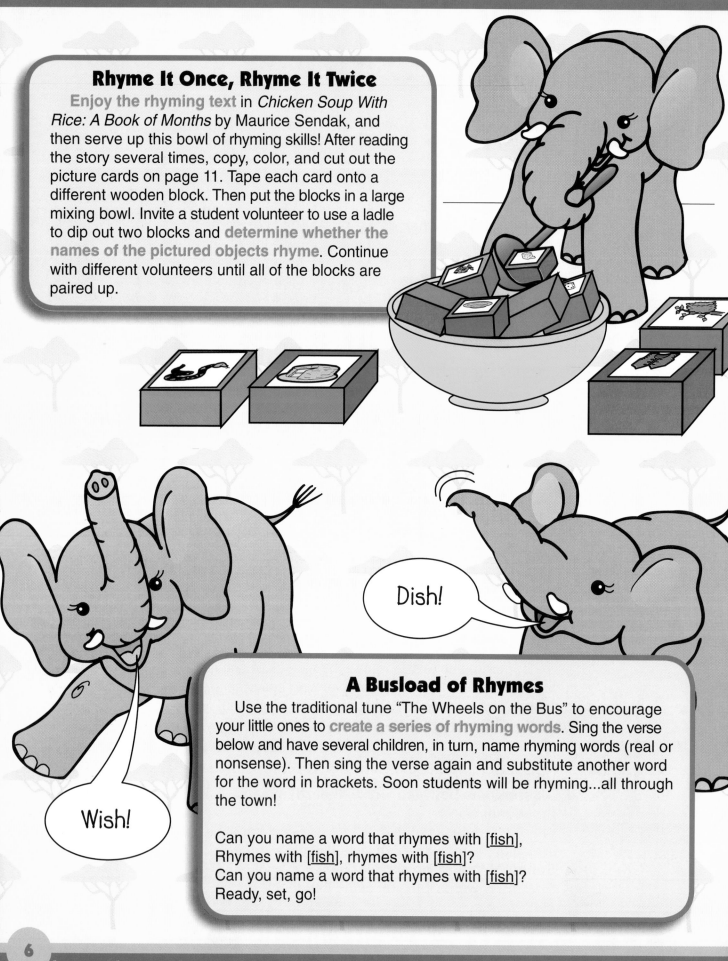

Rhyme It Once, Rhyme It Twice

Enjoy the rhyming text in *Chicken Soup With Rice: A Book of Months* by Maurice Sendak, and then serve up this bowl of rhyming skills! After reading the story several times, copy, color, and cut out the picture cards on page 11. Tape each card onto a different wooden block. Then put the blocks in a large mixing bowl. Invite a student volunteer to use a ladle to dip out two blocks and **determine whether the names of the pictured objects rhyme**. Continue with different volunteers until all of the blocks are paired up.

Dish!

Wish!

A Busload of Rhymes

Use the traditional tune "The Wheels on the Bus" to encourage your little ones to **create a series of rhyming words**. Sing the verse below and have several children, in turn, name rhyming words (real or nonsense). Then sing the verse again and substitute another word for the word in brackets. Soon students will be rhyming...all through the town!

Can you name a word that rhymes with [fish],
Rhymes with [fish], rhymes with [fish]?
Can you name a word that rhymes with [fish]?
Ready, set, go!

Jump or Slump?

Encourage youngsters to **discriminate between rhyming and nonrhyming words** with a simple transitional game that can be played whenever you have five minutes to spare. Call out a pair of words. If the words rhyme, have children jump up and down. If the words do not rhyme, have students slump and sink to the floor. It's fun, it's learning, *and* it gets the wiggles out!

Storytellers

Your students will help with the storytelling in this activity as they **listen, rhyme, and use oral language skills.** To begin, read aloud *Louella Mae, She's Run Away!* by Karen Beaumont Alarcón. After discussing the book, tell your students that you are going to read the selection again. This time, however, *they* are going to supply the rhyming words! Begin reading aloud. When you reach the second word of a rhyming pair, pause expectantly, waiting for children to complete the sentence. Afterward, try saying just the first word of a rhyming word pair. Can your youngsters think of its rhyme?

Did You Ever See...

It's read-along *and* sing-along time—in rhyme! To prepare, program a class supply of white construction paper with "Did you ever see a..." Gather your students and explore the rhythm and sounds in *Down by the Bay* from Raffi's collection of Songs to Read books (illustrated by Nadine Bernard Westcott). After sharing the book, teach the tune to your children and sing the song. Respond to the rhyming text by asking each child to think of an original imaginary rhyming scene that she might see at the bay. Have her draw and color her scene on a sheet of the programmed paper. Have the child write (or dictate as you write) to complete the rhyme. Then sing the song again, using your students' pages to complete the verses. You might even want to bind your students' pages to make a class book that they can read (and sing) over and over again!

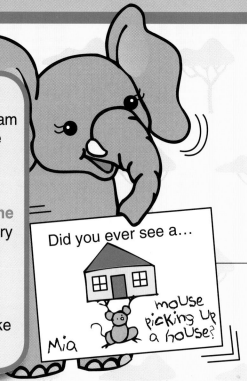

Hi-Ho, the Derry-O!

The *snake* is eating *cake?* The *cat* is really *fat?* Sure! In this rhyming song, anything goes! Sing a couple of verses of the song below to get your youngsters accustomed to how rhyming words can be substituted. Then have children name new rhyming word pairs and continue singing the song with their original verses. The *pie* in the *sky* is the limit!

(sung to the tune of "The Farmer in the Dell")

The [snake is eating cake].
The [snake is eating cake].
Hi-ho, the derry-o!
The [snake is eating cake].

Repeat the song, substituting new rhymes such as
 goat is in the boat
 soap is tied to rope
 girl likes to twirl
 boy broke the toy

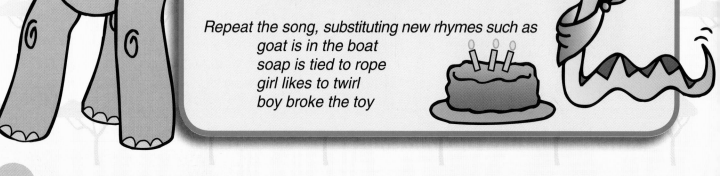

Lights Out!

Here's a flashy idea to entice students to **discriminate between rhyming and nonrhyming words**! First, make a darkened space by draping a large blanket or sheet over a long table. Ask a small group of youngsters to join you under the table; then give each of them a small flashlight. Have everyone turn on his flashlight. Direct the group to listen to you say a series of words. When the children hear a word that doesn't rhyme with the rest, they should flip off their flashlights! When the giggles subside, have everyone turn on his flashlight again; then begin with a new series of words.

car   tan

Let's play a game! I'm going to time it. I'll say a word and then you'll rhyme it!

Rhyme in Time

Invite your group to **create a series of rhyming words** as they race against the clock with this cooperative activity. Recite the verse on the left; then set a timer for 30 seconds or one minute (depending upon your group's abilities). Call out a word. Ask youngsters to name as many rhyming words as they can think of. Tally the words on your chalkboard until the timer rings and then count to see how many the group came up with. Try the same word again at another circle time to see if the group can improve its score. Or repeat the verse and name a new word for another rhyming race!

Pockets to Sock It!

What do you do anytime you find a rhyme? Sock it, with this idea! To prepare, glue each of several different pictures (use the cards on page 11 if desired) onto a separate white athletic sock as shown. Pin each sock to a bulletin board; then **treat your youngsters to the rhyming text** in *Fox in Socks* by Dr. Seuss. Once you get your tongue untwisted, direct your students' attention to the socks. Instruct them to **look in old magazines for any pictures whose names rhyme with those on the socks.** When a child identifies a rhyme, invite her to cut out the picture and place it in the corresponding sock. Revisit the socks frequently and have students **listen to the series of rhymes** that are forming. Then encourage youngsters to refer to the socks' contents when writing. This is yet another step toward phonological finesse!

The big pig wore a wig and danced a jig on a twig!

Picture This!

Get ready for lots of giggles as youngsters search for rhymes in these silly situations! Copy page 12 for each child. As a group, talk about the illustrations; then encourage each child to **identify and circle the rhyming objects or actions** depicted. As an extension, have the child illustrate her own rhyme on the back of her paper. Then invite her to share the rhyme with her classmates. Super-duper!

Picture Cards

Use with "Rhyme It Once, Rhyme It Twice" on page 6 and "Pockets to Sock It!" on page 10.

Picture This!

Note to the teacher: Use this page with "Picture This!" on page 10.

WORD AWARENESS

Use these ideas to get your young prereaders off and running with the knowledge of how their language works. It's true—words are wonderful!

Recognizing that *words, syllables,* and *phonemes* represent basic units of sound is fundamental in understanding our language structure because that's what our language is—a system of sounds! Word awareness is the initial (and easiest) stage of being phonologically aware.

The activities in this section will help your students do the following:

1 improve listening skills

2 recognize that words are units of sound within sentences

3 enjoy, engage in, and respond to literature that plays with language

4 develop new vocabulary

5 count the number of words in a sentence

Many opportunities to strengthen word awareness occur naturally throughout the day. When planning activities, keep the following tips in mind.

1. **Ask questions.**
   Asking children for predictions before reading and for conclusions after reading fosters vocabulary development and comprehension.

2. **Read it again and again!**
   Repeated readings seem to further youngsters' understanding of the language of the text. A child's retelling of a story becomes richer in language and meaning after multiple exposures to the text.

3. **Make connections to print.**
   Language experience charts and dictation are two common ways to expose children to the concept of a word. Through these activities, children see that talk can be written down, words are made up of different symbols, and words can be different lengths.

4. **Teach the alphabetic principle, too.**
   Phonological awareness training is more successful when combined with letter-name and letter-sound instruction.

What Do You See?

You've no doubt read Bill Martin Jr.'s *Brown Bear, Brown Bear, What Do You See?* many times. Use your youngsters' familiarity with the text to **encourage some oral language development**. Name a location, such as the park, the classroom, or the kitchen. Brainstorm with your youngsters a list of objects that can be found in this special location. Then have everyone chant the verse below, inviting each child to take a turn filling in the blank with an item of her choice. For more phonological awareness practice, use claps or slaps to **tap out the words in this rhythmic chant**.

Group: [Cassie, Cassie], what do you see?
Child: I see the [oven] looking at me!

I see the oven looking at me!

This is Beetza. He eats pizza.

Beetza

Tyler

That's Nonsense!

There's no better way to train little ears for the wonders of words than by entering the world of Dr. Seuss. Before reading aloud *One Fish, Two Fish, Red Fish, Blue Fish,* review the concept of reality versus fantasy. Tell your youngsters that there will be some imaginary creatures in the story. Instruct them to **listen as you read and to raise their hands when they hear an imaginary creature's name (a nonsense word)**. If desired, follow up the reading by inviting students to create their own wild and wacky creatures. Then have each child share his creature's nonsense name and something special about his picture. You'll soon have Gacks and Zanses and Yops all over your room!

Everyone Gets the Last Word

Use seasonal chants, poems, and songs to **reinforce phonological awareness word by word**. Pick a short verse (or use just a couple of lines from a longer one) that's catchy and fun for your students to say. For example, during the Christmas season, chant the first two lines of "Rudolph, the Red-Nosed Reindeer." Once everyone is familiar with it, start this elimination game. Help your group stand and form a circle. Designate one child to say the first word in the verse, the next child to say the second word, and so on. (When you come to the word *reindeer,* briefly explain that although *rein* and *deer* can be separate words, the animal name *reindeer* is one word.) Declare that the child who says the last word is the *first* Rudolph. Give her a red sticker for her nose and then direct her to sit down. Continue reciting the verse again and again until one child remains standing. Give him a sticker and have him lead the other reindeer in more reindeer games!

Other suggestions:

"Peter, Peter, Pumpkin Eater"—*each Peter gets a candy pumpkin*
"Twinkle, Twinkle, Little Star"—*sprinkle each eliminated star with glittery stardust*
"Hickory, Dickory, Dock"—*each mouse rings a chime to resemble the clock*
"Here Comes Peter Cottontail"—*each rabbit gets a jellybean*

Mary had a little fish!

Its skin was scaly and wet!

Mary Had a *What?*

Mary usually has a little lamb, but it's anybody's guess who or what will accompany her with this word awareness activity! To prepare, write the words to "Mary Had a Little Lamb" on chart paper, using blanks as shown below. After you **recite the traditional rhyme together, ask children to suggest substitutions for the word *lamb*.** Then say the rhyme together, including a substitute for *lamb*. When you get to the descriptive phrase at the end, ask the child who suggested the new word to orally fill in that blank.

Mary had a little _____, little _____, little _____.
Mary had a little _____. Its _____.

15

ss Word Awareness Word Awareness Word Awareness Word Awareness Word Awareness Wor
Awareness Word Awareness Word Awareness Word Awareness Word Awareness Word Awareness W

Word by Word

There will be lots of learning fun going on as your children **erase this favorite song word by word**. First, sing "Head, Shoulders, Knees, and Toes" together with the motions. Then sing the song again, but this time, don't sing the word *head;* just do the motion. Repeat the song, leaving off an additional word each time. If desired, use an enlarged copy of the patterns on page 18 to help students visually keep track of the song's words as they sing. Pretty soon your class will be "singing" the whole song in silent motion! What fun!

Sentence Building

Word awareness is going up fast at this construction site! To prepare, cut a supply of sentence strips into six-inch pieces. (You'll need several sets of about ten strips each.) To begin this group activity, say a simple sentence and ask your class to repeat it. Write each word of the sentence on a separate sentence strip piece. Then say the sentence again together, displaying one card for each word in the sentence. (Use your chalk ledge or a pocket chart.) Ask students to **count the cards to see how many words are in that sentence**. Ask students if they can add one word to the sentence. Write the suggested word on a sentence strip piece and insert it in the sentence. Say the sentence together again. Continue to **build the sentence as long as your students can supply additional words**.

big

The   dog   is   brown.

Name That Word

Roll out a little more practice in word awareness with this idea. During your Daily News or sharing time, record a student's dictated sentence on chart paper. Use a sentence with six words or less. Have your group **count the number of words aloud as you write the corresponding numeral under each word**. Practice reading the sentence together several times. Then give a volunteer a die and have her roll it. Instruct her to **identify the word in the sentence that matches the number on the die**. Continue in this manner with more volunteers. As youngsters' skills improve, stop numbering the words.

The Long and Short of It

Words come in many different sizes! Help youngsters grasp this idea by comparing the names of familiar animals. (This can be tricky because the size of an animal does not necessarily match the size of its name.) To prepare, cut out many different animal pictures. Glue each one to a separate sheet of tagboard. On the back of each tagboard piece, write the name of the animal.

To complete the activity, hold up pictures of two animals whose names are significantly different in length, such as a caterpillar and a horse. Have your students **name each animal and identify which animal's name is longer (or shorter)**. Once they agree on an answer, turn the pictures over to show the animals' names in print and then verify their answer. Continue in this manner for the rest of the pictures. As a challenge, occasionally put together two animals whose names are close to the same length and accept "the same" as the group's answer.

This activity could also incorporate your students' own pictures and names, or use other categories, such as food items, toys, and cartoon characters.

Patterns
Use with "Word by Word" on page 16.

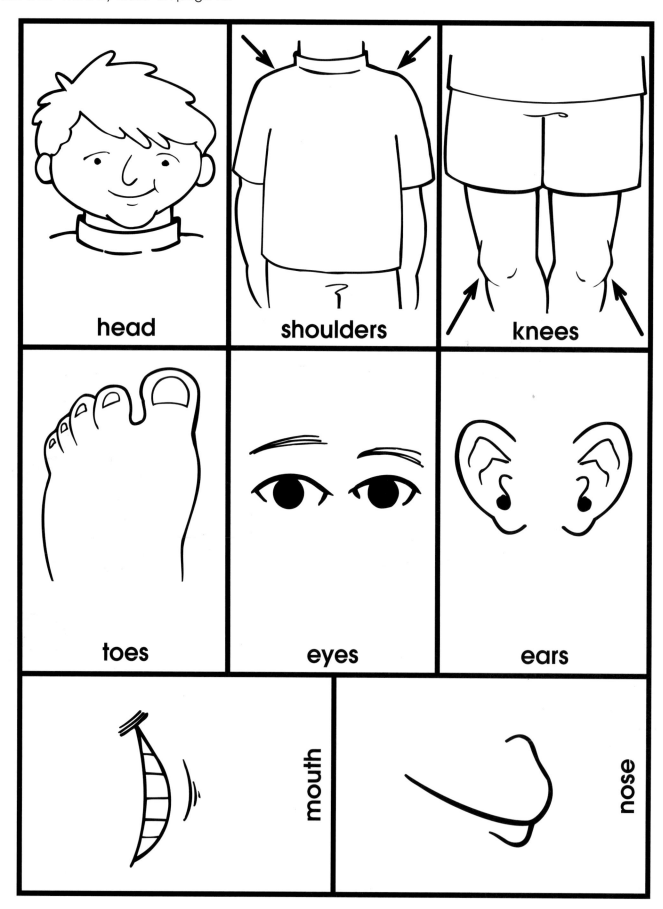

head

shoulders

knees

toes

eyes

ears

mouth

nose

PHONEME MATCHING

Before your young readers see too much black and white (text, that is), use the following oral activities to help them learn to listen for specific sounds in words.

A *phoneme* is the smallest unit of sound that matters in our language system. Once youngsters develop an understanding that words are made of individual phonemes, they can work on recognizing specific beginning, medial, or ending sounds in words.

The activities in this section will help your students do the following:

1 improve listening skills

2 explore the sounds of oral language

3 identify which word doesn't belong in a group of given words (oddity tasks)

4 enjoy, engage in, and respond to literature with alliterative text

5 categorize words containing the same beginning, medial, or ending sounds

6 name words that begin with a particular sound

Many opportunities to strengthen phoneme-matching skills occur naturally throughout the day. When planning activities, keep the following progression of skills (ordered from least difficult to most difficult) in mind. When working on positional sounds, beginning sounds are easiest, followed by ending sounds and then medial sounds.

1. **Know beginning and ending sounds.**
   B-B-Bat, b-b-bowl, b-b-big—what sound starts these words?
2. **Isolate and categorize sounds.**
   Cat, hot, bug, nut—which word does not have the same ending sound as the others?
   Can you put all of the pictures of items that start like *mouse* in a group?
3. **Supply sounds or words.**
   What is the last sound in the words *dig, rug, bag?*
   Name a word that ends with /t/.

Dazzling Diamonds

Direct your little darlings to divvy up a collection of "diamonds" as they **listen for the sound of** *d* **during a reading** of Pamela Duncan Edwards's *Dinorella: A Prehistoric Fairy Tale.* In advance, purchase a bag of plastic jewel shapes (for crafts) from your local discount store. Working with one small group of students at a time, place the jewels in the middle of the group. Slowly reread a passage from the book and instruct youngsters to take a diamond from the pile each time they hear a word that begins with the sound of *d.* After the reading, have students count their collections and see whether their totals match one another, as well as your correct number. As students return their diamonds to the pile, have them recall the *d* words they heard. Repeat the activity several times, reading a different passage each time. "Dino-mite!"

Kyle

Happy hippos hop around the beach.

Beach Fun for Everyone

What would happen if the zoo animals took a beach vacation? Ask your students to ponder this question as you read and **enjoy the alliterative text** in *Six Sandy Sheep* by Judith Ross Enderle. Afterward, call out a group of words from the story that begin with *s*. Ask students to **name the sound these words have in common.** Now give each child a sheet of paper and have him choose an animal from the zoo. Have the child describe the animal and tell what it does when it visits the beach—**using words that begin with the same sound as the animal's name.** For example, happy hippos might hop around the beach, or mischievous monkeys might march down the beach. Write each child's dictation on his paper and then have him illustrate his sentence. When youngsters have finished, invite them to share their work with their classmates.

He likes peas and potatoes!

Paul

What Do You Like?

Did you know that Paul likes *poodles* and *puppies,* but he does not like *dogs?* In this game, that's possible! To begin, ask one child to stand in front of the class. Have students say the chosen child's name as a group. Then call out a list of words, asking the class to **declare whether that child likes each item as it is mentioned.** If an item mentioned begins with the same sound as the child's name, he likes it. If not, he doesn't. Encourage older learners to **think of things the chosen child might like and not like, according to this sound formula.** Fun!

S-S-Simon S-S-Says

This special version of the game Simon Says calls for good listening ears! Tell your students that in this game, Simon wants them to **perform only the actions in which the main words start with the same sound**, such as "touch your tummy." If the requested action doesn't contain at least two of the same initial sounds, have your youngsters say, "Simon wouldn't say that!" To extend this activity, encourage your children to think of commands that S-S-Simon might give.

S-S-Suggestions for S-S-Simon:
Touch your tummy.
Hop high.
Wiggle your waist.
Lift your leg.
Tap your toes.
Knock your knees.
Nod your head. *(Simon wouldn't say that!)*
Shake your shoulders.
Hold your hands high.
Sing a song.
March a minute.

Wiggle my fingers...

Simon wouldn't say that!

Jumping Jacks and Jills

Jump right into letter sounds with an activity that builds muscles as it builds phonological awareness! To prepare, arrange three to five carpet squares in a winding path. Working with one small group at a time, explain that each student will **travel down the path by naming words that have the same beginning sound as a given word**. To begin, say a word, such as *bug,* for the first child. When he names a word with the same beginning sound, such as *bed,* have him jump onto the first square. Encourage him to keep naming words with matching beginning phonemes and jumping onto subsequent squares until he reaches the end of the path. Then give the next child a new word to take on her jumping journey.

Bed!

"Al-literally" Speaking...

Explore alliterative language during your thematic studies with this class book idea. Select a sentence frame that corresponds with your unit of study. (See the list below for some possibilities.) Write the frame on a sentence strip, leaving space for each missing word. Read the sentence aloud, filling in the blanks with alliterative words to give students an example. Together, brainstorm a list of other examples. Then have each child **use the frame to dictate an alliterative sentence to you**. Write his sentence on a tagboard strip; then have him illustrate his sentence on an index card. Glue his illustration to the end of his sentence. After everyone has completed a sentence and drawing, bind the strips as shown to make a class book. Read the entire book aloud and then keep it in the reading area for further enjoyment. What a wild and wonderful way to work with words!

Possible sentence frames:
garden theme
[Marie] grows [magnificent mushrooms] in the garden.
[Daniel] grows [delightful daisies] in the garden.
zoo theme
The [lion] eats [lots of lemon licorice].
The [baboon] eats [bananas on buttered buns].
farm theme
There's a [cute, colorful cow catching carrots] in the barnyard.
There's a [perky, pink pig picking up pennies] in the barnyard.
transportation theme
A [tooting taxi] is traveling to [Tennessee].
A [shapely ship] is traveling to [the shore].
community helpers theme
The [polite policeman] helps by [pointing to people].
The [busy banker] helps by [bundling bills].

There's a curious cat counting cakes in the barnyard.

Sorting Through Sounds

Gadgets, gizmos, trinkets, toys—all of them can be used to help children **focus on the sounds found in words**. In advance, copy the note on page 25 for each child. Once you have collected a nice variety of objects, arrange them in rows (use the number of objects that's appropriate for your group) and gather a small group of students around them. Call out a directive for each child. For example, say "Find an object that starts with /b/." Encourage the child to **pick up the specified object and say its name**. After working with beginning sounds, try ending sounds and then medial sounds. As an extension, show a group of objects in which all but one object has an ending sound in common (for example, a pe**n**, a ca**n**, a su**n**, and a ca**t**). Challenge students to **pick out the object that doesn't belong**. Continue until each child has had several turns.

Whose House?

This learning center idea will provide some "homework" as youngsters practice phoneme-matching skills. To prepare, cut out four or more magazine pictures or clip-art illustrations, each representing a different short-vowel medial sound. Glue each picture to a separate 3" x 5" index card. Now, for each group of pictures, draw a simple house shape (similar to the one shown) on a large sheet of construction paper. Make each room's size match a 3" x 5" card. Label each house with one of the different medial sounds represented. Glue one picture from each group onto the appropriate house to serve as examples. Then laminate all of the houses and cards for durability. To complete the activity, have a child **place each picture card in its correct house according to its medial sound**. This activity could also be modified to practice beginning or final sounds. Ah…home, sweet home!

Full Steam Ahead

Load up on phoneme-matching skills with this traveling train! Pick one child to be the engineer and have her hold a large card programmed with the letter or letters that represent a beginning sound of your choice. Direct her to repeat the sound as she chugs around the room. Next, have her stop at a classmate's seat to allow him to join the train. His "ticket" to board is **naming a word that begins with the engineer's sound**. After the two link, encourage them to travel to another passenger. Continue until there are five to ten passengers; then choose a new engineer and a new beginning sound. Choo! Choo!

Shop 'Til You Drop

Invite your youngsters to go on a shopping spree using their names as cash! To prepare, copy page 26 for each child and then gather a supply of old magazines, scissors, and glue. Give each child a page and have him write his name on it where indicated. Direct him to look through the magazines and **cut out pictures of objects that have the same beginning or ending sound as his name**. Have the child sort these pictures on his page according to their matching sounds. Review his work and then have him glue the pictures to the page. Encourage youngsters to share their great buys with the group; then display their pages on a bulletin board titled "Savvy Shoppers." Learning to discriminate the sounds in words—*priceless!*

Gotta Get a Gadget!

Dear Parents,

    We need your help! We're working on recognizing certain matching sounds in words and need a big collection of objects to explore. Please look through your "catchall" drawers at home (we all have them!) and send in any small gadgets, gizmos, trinkets, or toys that you'd like to get rid of. Misplaced game pieces, kid's meal toys, craft items, plastic miniature figures, cake decorations, small household items, and other novelties would be great! We really appreciate your participation and will be looking for your donations by _____.

Thanks!

Gotta Get a Gadget!

Dear Parents,

    We need your help! We're working on recognizing certain matching sounds in words and need a big collection of objects to explore. Please look through your "catchall" drawers at home (we all have them!) and send in any small gadgets, gizmos, trinkets, or toys that you'd like to get rid of. Misplaced game pieces, kid's meal toys, craft items, plastic miniature figures, cake decorations, small household items, and other novelties would be great! We really appreciate your participation and will be looking for your donations by _____.

Thanks!

©The Education Center, Inc. • *Phonological Awareness Fun* • TEC488

Note to the teacher: Use with "Sorting Through Sounds" on page 23.

Shop 'Til You Drop

_____
(your name)

These things have some of the same sounds as my name. I'll take 'em!

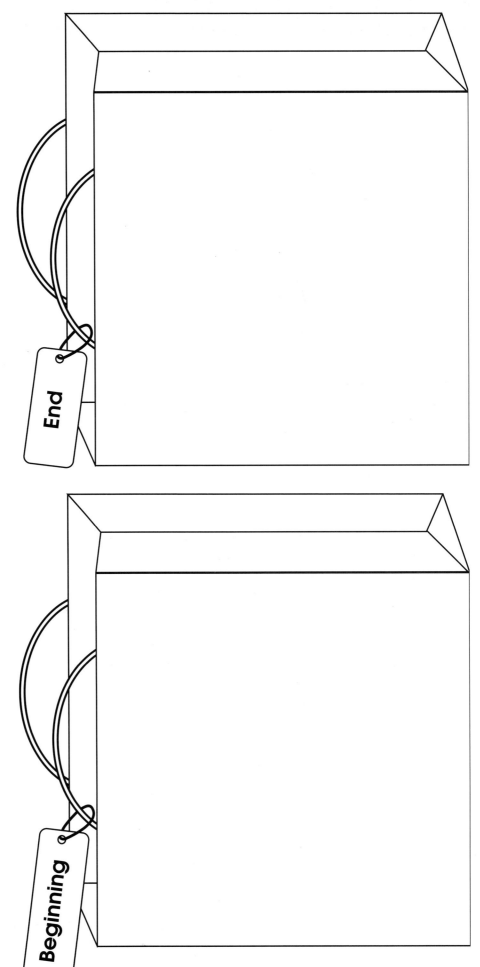

End

Beginning

Note to the teacher: Use with "Shop 'Til You Drop" on page 24.

BLENDING

It's time to encourage youngsters to stick out their necks and try a new skill—blending sounds to make words. It's well within reach when you use the ideas found here!

Blending is the skill of pronouncing the sounds of a word together. Because blending and segmenting are complementary processes, it can be beneficial to use both types of activities during the same time frame. Research has shown that these two phonological skills are very important prerequisites to beginning reading instruction.

The activities in this section will help your students do the following:

1 combine two words to make a compound word

2 combine syllables to make a word

3 combine an onset and rime to make a word

4 combine phonemes to make a word

5 use manipulatives to illustrate blending sounds into words

Many opportunities to strengthen blending skills occur naturally throughout the day. When planning blending activities, keep the following teaching tips in mind.

1. **Model.**
   Be sure to pronounce words and sounds slowly and even exaggerate the pronunciation.
2. **Work from easier tasks to more difficult skills.**
   Start with compound words; then move to syllables, onsets and rimes, and phonemes. Fricatives *(s, v, f)* are easier to blend than stop consonants *(p, b, t, d)*.
3. **Give visual cues.**
   Write two word parts on separate cards; then move the cards together as you continue to blend them into one word.

27

Blending Blending Blending Blending Blending Blending Blending Blending Blending Blending B
ding Blending Blending Blending Blending Blending Blending Blending Blending Blendin

Compounds Abound

Play this quick and easy game with a small group to **practice blending pairs of picture words into compound words**. To prepare, make a copy of page 34 on construction paper and then cut the cards apart. Arrange the cards faceup on a tabletop. Provide a pointer for children to use.

To play, seat several children around the table and give the pointer to the first player. Call out a pair of words from the list. Ask the player to point to the picture word that can be made from the two words and then say it. Discuss with the child how he made his decision. Have the player pass the pointer to the next child, and continue playing until each compound word is identified.

Word Pairs for Compound

tooth	paste
skate	board
flower	pot
lady	bug
flash	light
air	plane
note	book
butter	fly
foot	print

A Blending Boa

No need to fear this snake! It only constricts to **produce compound words**! To **make the snake manipulative**, insert a Slinky toy into a dark-colored kneesock. Stretch the sock and the Slinky so that the toe of the sock fits snugly around one end of the Slinky. Tuck the sock's opening into the other end of the Slinky. Add two wiggle eyes and a red felt tongue, and the boa is ready to blend!

Use a copy of page 35 to create picture word cards. Tape a pair of corresponding cards to opposite ends of the snake as shown. Pull the snake apart as much as possible and say each picture word. Then slowly push the snake together while children chorally and repeatedly say the words with less and less silence between them. Finally, when the cards meet, pronounce the compound word that the two words form. Continue in this manner with more compound words.

Seeing Stars

Have your students pretend to be stargazers as they **practice blending syllables**. Affix glow-in-the-dark stars to several different classroom objects with multisyllabic names. Darken the room as much as possible and turn on a flashlight. Say the modified rhyme below, inserting a student's name. Pick one of the starred objects in the room and say its name, exaggerating the breaks between syllables. Give the flashlight to the chosen student. Encourage her to blend the syllables together and shine the "starlight" on the corresponding object. Repeat the process, inserting a different child's name in the rhyme each time. A teacher's wish comes true—learning that's motivating and fun!

Star light, star bright,
[Kayleigh], it's *you* I will invite!
Listen close with all your might.
Can you say this word just right?
[Sta-pler].

Cookin' Up Words

Who's the best phonological gourmet around? You are when you involve your little chefs in blending these recipes! To prepare, gather a mixing bowl, a large spoon, a bell, a foil pie pan, and up to six manipulatives. Put on a chef's hat and an apron.

Explain that you'd like to bake some words, but you need help. Tell students that you have the ingredients for the recipes, but you don't know what the recipes actually make! Choose a student volunteer to help you with the first concoction. (If desired, provide a hat or an apron for him.) **Pick a multi-syllabic food word and pronounce each syllable as you put a manipulative in the bowl**. Next, have the child stir the ingredients for a few seconds. As he stirs, encourage the class to softly chant the syllables. When the child has **blended the syllables and identified the word**, have him ring the bell—it's ready! Have the child dump the ingredients into the pie pan and announce what word has been made. Repeat the activity in this manner until everyone has had a turn. Then reward your chefs with real treats, such as cookies or muffins!

All in the Family

This activity is just the ticket to **reinforce onset and rime blending skills**! Plan to use familiar rimes, such as -at, with different onsets (such as /b/, /m/, and /s/) that when paired with -at will make words. To do this activity, choose a child to say the first rime. Tell him that every time you point to him, he is to say /at/. Next, choose a volunteer to say an onset, such as /m/, and direct him to stand a few paces away from the other child. As you point to each child, have him say his sound(s). Then have them move a little closer together. Do this several times and point faster with each exchange until the onset and rime are smoothly blended and the children are shoulder to shoulder. Then ask the whole class to say the entire word—*mat!* Continue this activity with as many different onsets as you'd like. Then, on another day, blend with a new rime. (Refer to the list at the right for suggestions.) It's time to blend with a friend!

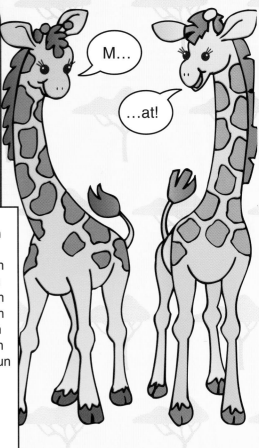

-at	-en	-in	-ot	-un
bat	den	bin	cot	bun
cat	hen	fin	dot	fun
fat	men	kin	hot	nun
hat	pen	pin	lot	pun
mat	ten	tin	pot	run
pat	then	win	rot	sun
rat	when	chin	tot	spun
sat		grin		
		shin		
		skin		
		thin		
		twin		

Green and Red

Green means "go" and red means "stop," right? Right! Take advantage of these universal color signals to help build blending skills. Working with a small group of children, give each child in the group (and yourself) a green block and a red block. Have each person set her green block on the left and her red block on the right. Tell children that each word you say has two parts and will start with the green block and end with the red block. For example, say, "Green says /s/…" and push the green block out to your left. Then say, "…and red says /ee/" as you push the red block to your right. Have each child repeat the sounds and movements with her own blocks. Then, in unison, **move the blocks slowly back together as you blend the two sounds**. When the blocks touch, say the whole word. Repeat this activity with other two-phoneme words. There's no stopping now!

Who's Next?

Try this clever chant to **practice blending skills** during your next transition time. Choose a student, split his name into syllables, and insert it in the chant where indicated. Have each child **listen for his name and line up when he recognizes it**. To make the activity a little more challenging, occasionally call out syllables that form a name similar to, but different from, one of the students' names. Continue until everyone's name is called. For added fun, make a pair of binoculars to use to spot those who are ready to move on to the next activity. To make a pair, simply staple two toilet paper tubes together and attach a piece of string as shown. The more drama, the better—let's go!

> Who's next? Who's next?
> I'm looking for the one.
> Who will be the next child
> Ready for some fun?
> It's [Ray-mond]! Line up, please.

> To market, to market,
> to buy a black
> sh-eep!

> Sh-eep,
> sheep!

To Market, to Market

Engage your students in a storytime guessing game that uses their blending skills. To prepare, obtain a copy of the book *To Market, to Market* by Anne Miranda. As you read the first half of the story aloud, don't show the pictures. When you come to an animal name, segment it into its onset and rime (or into its individual phonemes). Invite youngsters to **blend the word together**. Then show the picture to confirm their answer and finish the rhyme. Once all of the animals are introduced, finish reading the story as you normally would.

Picture Pickers

Picture this: students excited and anxious to **practice blending phonemes into words**. It can happen with this game! To prepare, duplicate page 36 and cut apart the picture word cards.

Gather a small group of students at a table and then place two or three picture word cards in the middle of the table. Call out the individual phonemes of one of the pictured objects. Encourage the children to blend the sounds together to figure out the word. Pass the picture word card to the first child who identifies it. Then add a new picture word card to the bunch and play another round, having the child who received the last picture word card sit out the next round.

Teacher's Pet

Here's a quick activity to **reinforce onset and rime blending skills**. In advance, store a supply of small stuffed animals in your circle area, making sure each animal's name is a monosyllabic word with a simple onset-rime construction, such as *fish, cat, rat, dog, bird,* and *pig.* Next, gather your group and show them the animals. Ask students to listen for part of a pet name. Then secretly choose the name of a stuffed animal and say its rime. Ask a volunteer to **identify the beginning sound that goes before the rime** to name one of the animals. Have the child repeatedly say the initial sound before you say the rime, each time making a more complete blend until the word is clearly apparent. Afterward, have her select, name, and hold the matching stuffed animal. Repeat the game with a new animal each time, continuing as long as interest dictates.

Put It All Together

A little music goes a long way when it comes to phonological awareness! Sing the song below slowly to your students. At the end of the song, ask your class to **blend the sounds together and pronounce the word.** (For younger children, you might ask them to first repeat the song before blending the sounds together.) Once your students have the hang of it, invite individual children or small groups of children to **sing the song using any other three-phoneme words.** Fun—/f/-/u/-/n/!

(sung to the tune of "London Bridge")

What word sounds like /c/-/a/-/t/, /c/-/a/-/t/, /c/-/a/-/t/?
What word sounds like /c/-/a/-/t/?
Can you say it?
Cat!

Blending Cheer

Remember that old call-and-response cheer where the cheerleaders shout, "I say, 'Number.' You say, 'One.' Number…" and the audience responds with a loud, rousing "One!" Well, how about pepping up your classroom blending activities with a variation of that same cheer? You can use any two-phoneme word. After each round of the cheer, encourage your students to **blend the two parts together and shout out the entire word.** If desired, give out pom-poms and *really* rev it up!

Teacher: I say /m/. You say /e/.
Teacher: /m/
Class: /e/
Teacher: /m/
Class: /e/
Teacher: /m/
Class: /e/

Everyone shouts: Me!

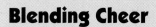

Picture Word Cards

Use with "Compounds Abound" on page 28.

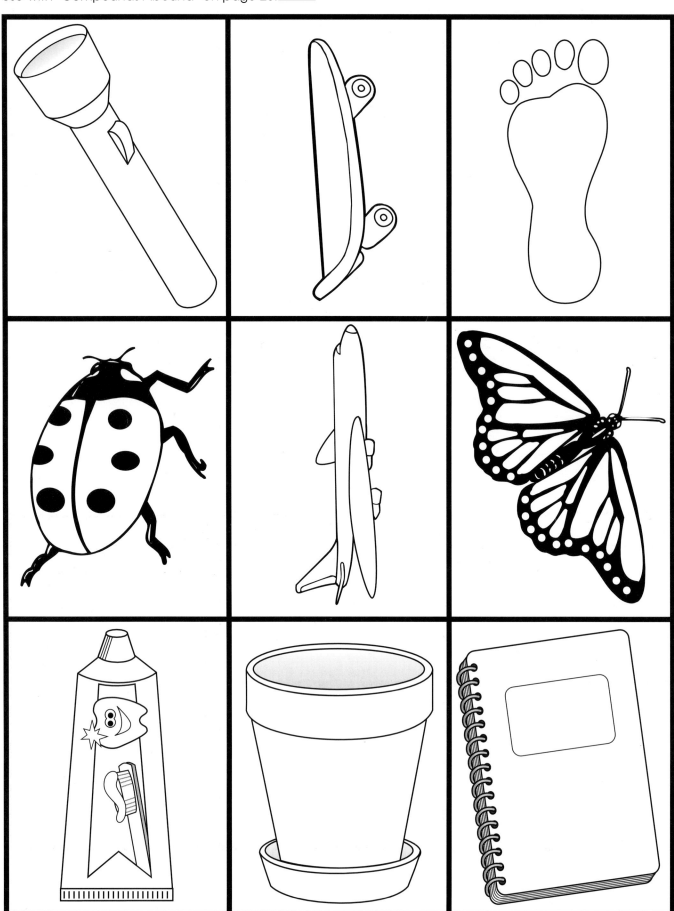

©The Education Center, Inc. • *Phonological Awareness Fun* • TEC488

Key

Answers may vary.
Possible answers
include the following:

doghouse
watchdog
birdhouse
cowbell
doorbell
cowboy
cowgirl
cowhand

Picture Word Cards
Use with "Picture Pickers" on page 32.

SEGMENTING

These activities will help your cubs learn how to segment words into syllables and syllables into sounds. Learning to read is going to be gr-r-r-reat!

Segmenting is a phonological skill of moderate difficulty. As children learn to separate the sounds in words, they can better understand how alphabet letters correspond to these sounds.

The activities in this section will help your students do the following:

1 separate words into syllables

2 count how many syllables or sounds

3 separate syllables (or one-syllable words) into sounds

4 isolate the initial sound from the rest of a syllable

5 use manipulatives, such as plastic counters, to represent the sounds in a word

6 make connections between letters and sounds

Many opportunities to strengthen segmenting skills occur naturally throughout the day. When planning activities, keep the following progression of skills in mind (ordered here from least difficult to most difficult). When working on phonemes, note that fricatives (such as *f, s, v, z*) and vowels are easier for students to segment than stop consonants (such as *p, b, t, d*).

1. **Sentence Level**
   Clap for each word in this sentence: This is my car.
2. **Compound Word Level**
   Clap for each smaller word you hear in *pancake.*
3. **Syllable Level**
   How many word parts are in the word *letter?*
4. **Onset and Rime Level**
   What is the first sound you hear in *ship?*
5. **Phonemic Level**
   What three sounds are in the word *cat?*

37

Word Parts

Counting syllables is melodious in this easy song. Teach the verse below to your students. Then, after singing the tune together, name a word. Have a volunteer repeat the word, clap its "parts," and **tell how many syllables it has**. If she is correct, invite her to call out a word in the next round of play. If she is incorrect, repeat the word, clap its parts, and help her count the syllables. Ready, set, sing!

(sung to the tune of "Did You Ever See a Lassie?")

Can you count how many word parts,
The word parts, the word parts?
Can you count how many word parts
You hear in this word?

> ## mit-ten
> Mitten has two parts.

Gin-ger-bread!

Use this idea to cook up some fun with segmenting skills. To prepare, cut out a class supply of gingerbread man shapes from construction paper or craft foam. (Or use sheets from a gingerbread man–shaped notepad.) Also purchase a bag of small cinnamon candies to serve as the gingerbread men's buttons. Give each child a gingerbread man and a few candies.

To complete the activity, call out a word containing one to four syllables (see below for suggestions). Have each child repeat the word and then **place buttons on her gingerbread man to correspond with the correct number of syllables in the word**. Continue in this manner for several rounds. Then start again with a new round of words.

Possible word categories:
baking or cooking words
names of different cookies
fairy-tale words
Christmas words

Burger Bites

It's time to supersize students' work on syllables! Copy the hamburger pattern (page 45) onto construction paper for each child. Direct the child to use crayons to color his pattern and then have him cut it out. Use a dark-colored permanent marker to write each child's first name on his burger. Then provide scallop-cut scissors for the student to use to cut the appropriate number of bites out of his burger to **show how many syllables are in his name**. Have each child find a partner whose burger has the same number of bites; use the burgers to make a class graph; or mount the burgers on a bulletin board with a catchy title.

Having a Ball!

Enjoy Junie and Jakie's "lumpety bumpety" trip to the lake in *Rattletrap Car* by Phyllis Root; then use a beach ball to bounce into some phonological awareness fun. Have your students stand and form a circle. Call out a one-syllable word from the story and pass the ball to someone. Direct that child to repeat your word, bounce the ball twice as she **splits the word into its onset and rime**, and pass the ball back to you. Then repeat the round using another word with a different child. For added fun, invite each child who segments your word correctly to "dive" into the middle of the lake (the circle) and swim around for a few seconds. Aahhh…so refreshing!

b-all

l-ake

39

Fun, Compounded

This segmenting activity is sure to engage and delight your little ones! To begin, seat students in a circle and give each child a pair of connected linking cubes. Next, explain to students that they will listen to a word and then break it into its two separate, smaller words. Say a simple compound word, making sure each part of the word is one syllable (see the list below for suggestions). Have students **say the word with you and then segment it into its component syllables as they separate their cubes,** holding one in each hand. Encourage students to say each word segment while holding one cube in each hand. (If desired, invite students to repeatedly say the segments faster and faster as they blend the word together and reconnect the cubes.) Continue segmenting words in this manner, adding new compound words as desired. Awe-some!

Compound Words

cowboy	cupcake	pancake
daytime	birthday	railroad
bedroom	bookcase	snowflake
teaspoon	shoelace	cookbook

What's in a Name?

Here's a segmenting idea for centers. To prepare, photocopy four to six children's individual photos onto the same sheet of paper. Repeat this process until each child appears on a page. Then make several copies of each page. Arrange a new set of pages and some pencils in a center each day.

To do this activity, have a child say the name of one of the pictured children. Instruct her to **draw a tally mark under the child's photo for each syllable in that name.** Then have her count the total number of tally marks, write the number down, and circle it. Have her continue in this manner until each child's name on the page has been segmented.

Gather and Graph

Combine segmenting with graphing skills to create this educational experience. To prepare, write each number from one to six on a different index card. Arrange the cards in a grid on the floor to serve as graph labels. Working with a small group of children, ask each child in the group to pick up a small object from your classroom and bring it back to the group. In turn, have each child show his object and say its name. Then have the group **repeat the name slowly, clapping as each syllable is said.** As the group claps, encourage the child who has shown the object to count the number of claps. Then have him **put his object in the graph according to the number of syllables in its name.** Discuss what the graph reveals. Won-der-ful!

Hand to Hand

All hands must be on deck for this activity, in which each child will **segment the initial sound from the rest of the word.** To begin, call out a one-syllable word to your class, such as *dog.* Have the class repeat the word once. Then have each child extend her left hand and say just the onset of the word—/d/. Then have her extend her right hand and say the rime—/og/. Finally, have her extend both hands at the same time and say the complete word—*dog.* Repeat this activity with as many words as you like.

/d/    /og/    /dog/

Heads Up!

Head, tummy, toes—they are body segments, so why not use them to actively segment words? Show students a picture word card (such as the ones from page 46). Encourage each child to think about the picture word and listen as you say its name aloud. Invite each child to **repeat the word, touching her head as she says the beginning sound, her tummy as she says the middle sound, and her toes as she says the ending sound**. Repeat the activity with a different picture word card each time. Go ahead and get those wiggles out!

Oh, Do You Know?

Tune into segmented sounds with this simple song. Seat students in a circle and sing the verse at the right, holding up a different picture word card each time you sing and inserting the word in the song. (The picture word cards on page 46 may be used for this purpose.) Encourage the child sitting next to you to **make the beginning, middle, and ending sounds of your designated word**. Sing the song again, this time asking the same child to choose a picture word card for the song's final line. Then have the child's neighbor provide the appropriate sounds of his word while his classmates silently think of the sounds they hear. Repeat the activity, going around the circle so that each child has a turn to provide sounds and a new word for the song. Yes, we know our phoneme sounds!

(sung to the tune of "The Muffin Man")

Oh, do you know the phoneme sounds,
The phoneme sounds, the phoneme sounds?
Oh, do you know the phoneme sounds
Of the word [*hat*]?

Flip Strips

Your youngsters will flip over this activity, in which they will practice segmenting with onsets and rimes. To prepare, fold several sheets of construction paper in half lengthwise. Inside each sheet's fold (bottom half), write a different one-syllable vocabulary word from your current teaching unit. Then cut the top half of the paper so that once it's refolded, the onset and rime are separated as shown. During circle time, show students one of the words. Read it aloud; then model orally and visually how to **segment the word into its onset and rime**. Repeat this process with another word, giving students the chance to chime in. Continue until each word has been segmented. To provide more practice, place a supply of paper, a list of one-syllable words (CVC words, such as *sit, mud,* and *dog* are preferable at first), markers, and scissors in the literacy center and invite youngsters to make their own flip strips. What a great tip!

Step Right Up!

Take segmenting skills to the stairway with this small-group game. To play, position four students side by side at the bottom of a short, wide flight of stairs. Stand at the top of the stairs and call out a word (such as *mad, rip,* or *ship*) for the first child. Have him **climb a step as he pronounces each sound of the word**. If the child answers correctly, he stays on the step he ended with. If his response is incorrect, say the word again, exaggerating each sound and marching in place with the child to indicate each separate sound. Ask him to step back one step. Continue in this manner until everyone makes it to the top of the stairs.

s-ee-d

Flower Power

Watch youngsters' segmenting skills reach full bloom with this idea! Purchase a package of inexpensive, flower-shaped butter cookies. Have each child color a grass line and draw five empty flower stems on a 4½" x 12" strip of construction paper. Give each youngster five cookies and then call out a word from the list at the right. Have each child **put a flower cookie on a stem to represent each sound she hears as she repeats the word, elongating its sounds**. Continue in this manner for each of the words on the list (or other words of your choice). This idea can also be modified by using holiday-shaped cookies and holiday words, sea animal–shaped crackers and ocean-themed words, or other similar products—anything to get young minds growing!

Word List

sun	seed	dig
stem	rain	hoe
root	bud	bloom
grow	leaf	plant

Sound Off!

Motivate your young reading recruits to **separate words into sounds** with this catchy cadence! Have students repeat the lines as noted. If desired, march around the room while chanting to add movement and rhythm. Challenge older students to **come up with more four-phoneme words to segment**; otherwise, provide words as desired. The incentive here? If *you* think of a word, *you* get to lead the troops!

Teacher: Listen up! Now have you heard?
Students: Listen up! Now have you heard?
Teacher: We know how to sound out words.
Students: We know how to sound out words.
Teacher: Let's give the word *[snake]* a try.
Students: Let's give the word *[snake]* a try.
Teacher: Join right in; now don't be shy!
Students: Join right in; now don't be shy!

Teacher: Sound off!
Everyone: [/s/ /n/]
Teacher: Sound off!
Everyone: [/a/ /k/]
Teacher: Break it on down!
Everyone: [/s/ /n/ /a/ /k/, /s/ /n/ /a/ /k/]!

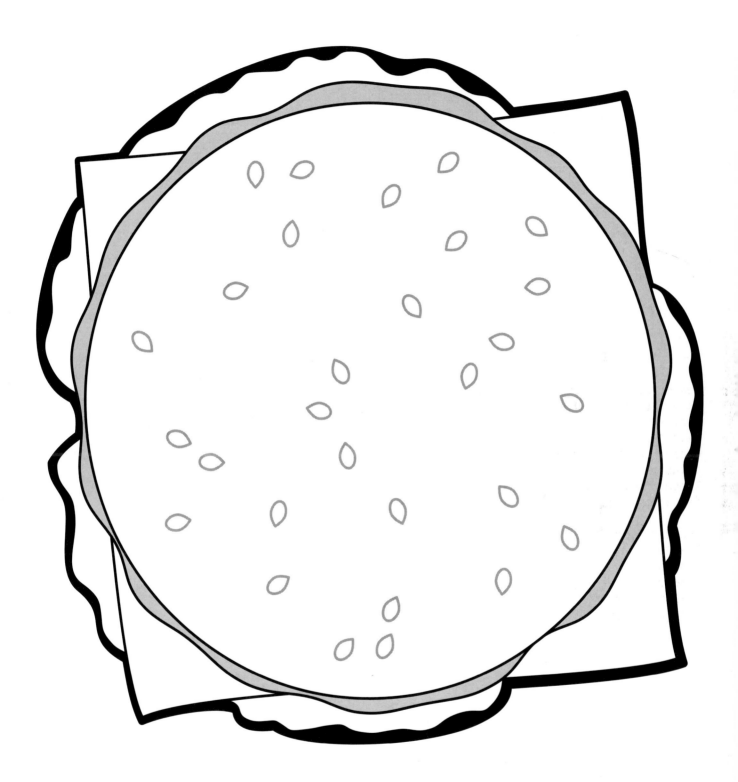

Picture Word Cards

Use with "Heads Up!" and "Oh, Do You Know?" on page 42.

PHONEME MANIPULATION

Now that your students have practiced their rhyming, matching, segmenting, and blending skills, go bananas with ideas that focus on phoneme manipulation.

The most difficult phonological awareness level, phoneme awareness, includes the task of phoneme manipulation. This simply means that sounds are added to, deleted from, or substituted in a word in order to make new words. Students should be well versed in (but not necessarily have mastered) rhyming, matching, segmenting, and blending before attempting this level of skill. Because phoneme manipulation requires a lot of strength in the easier phoneme awareness skills, most children should not be expected to independently manipulate phonemes before the very end of the first grade. Children attempting to manipulate phonemes prior to that will need lots of teacher support.

The activities in this section will help your students do the following:

1 replace the initial, final, and medial sounds of words to make new words

2 add sounds to an existing word to make new words

3 enjoy and respond to literature that plays phonemically with the text

4 use concrete objects to illustrate manipulating sounds within words

5 make connections between letters and sounds

Many opportunities to strengthen phoneme manipulation skills occur naturally throughout the day. When planning activities, keep the following teaching tips in mind.

1. **Be explicit.**
   While these activities are fun and engaging, be sure to intentionally focus on the sound structure of the words.
2. **Progress from easier to more difficult tasks.**
   Working with initial and final sounds is easier than working with medial sounds.
3. **Begin to bring in letter-sound correspondence.**
   When using manipulatives, label them with letters, if possible, to increase exposure to the letter-sound connection without focusing on letter names.

47

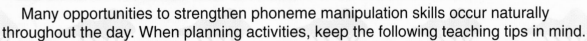
oneme Manipulation   Phoneme Manipulation   Phoneme Manipulation   Phoneme Manipulation   hen
me Manipulation   Phoneme Manipulation   Phoneme Manipulation   Phoneme Manipulation   Phoneme Ma

What's on the Menu?

Youngsters will "eat up" this dramatic-play activity as they **replace the initial sounds of words to cook up some new words**! Use a few props to create a restaurant table in your classroom. Sit at the table with a small group of students. Ask one child to stand up and pretend to be the server. If desired, give him an apron, an order pad, and a pen or pencil. When he asks for your order, request one or more common food items, but replace the beginning sound of a word with another sound. For example, you might say, "I'd like a **j**amburger and **sh**ies, please." Encourage the server to decode and repeat your order: "Yes, of course, a hamburger and fries!" Give every child in the group a chance to play the server and take your order.

As students improve, take the activity to a new level by asking each child at the table to place a silly order of her own. Continue until every child has once again had a chance to play the server. Bank you! Some again!

No, no, no! That's all wrong! This is the way to sing that song...

That Song's All Wrong!

Put a musical twist on phoneme manipulation with an activity that incorporates familiar tunes. Sing a line or two of a favorite children's song, such as "Mary Had a Little Lamb," but **replace an initial, medial, or final sound in one of the words**. For example, you might sing, "Mary had a little lumb." Teach little ones to respond by calling out the chant shown when they hear a mistake. Invite the child or children who call out the chant to then sing the line of the song correctly for the class. Discuss the incorrect word and how it is different in sound from the correct one. Soon, you'll be hearing strange, new versions of tunes as students experiment on their own. Wrinkle, wrinkle, little star...

Merrily, Merrily

Giggles and grins will accompany this merry little activity, in which students help **change initial sounds in words to make new words**. To begin, sing "Row, Row, Row Your Boat" with your class. Then ask a child to name a specific sound, such as the first sound in her name, her favorite letter's sound, or the sound of a specific letter of the alphabet. Now help your students sing the song again, replacing the /r/ in each *row* and/or the /m/ in each *merrily* with the chosen sound. What a way to rock the boat!

Example for /d/:
Dow, dow, dow your boat
Gently down the stream.
Derrily, derrily, derrily, derrily
Life is but a dream.

Switcheroo!

This lively card game provides youngsters with an opportunity to **practice replacing the phonemes in different parts of words to make new words**. In advance, photocopy the picture cards on pages 53 and 54. Color, laminate, and then cut apart the cards. To begin, seat a small group of children in a circle and then divide the picture cards among them. Have one child show one of her cards and tell what it is (for example, "boat"). Next, designate a word part—beginning, middle, or end—and ask her to give a sound to replace the corresponding sound in the word (for example, "/g/ for the beginning sound"). Then encourage the whole group to say the new word (real or nonsense) together. Repeat this process until each child has shown all of her cards.

49

Phoneme Manipulation   Phoneme Manipulation   Phoneme Manipulation   Phoneme Manipulation
Phoneme Manipulation   Phoneme Manipulation   Phoneme Manipulation   Phoneme Manipulation

That Old Man!

The old man's back, and this time he's giving youngsters a chance to **make new words by replacing initial sounds** in his song lyrics. Sing the original version of "This Old Man" together. Then name a letter sound to use in the verse below. If desired, write the new lyrics on sentence strips and put them in a pocket chart to **reinforce connections between letters and sounds**. Repeat the verse several times with different consonant sounds or blends. Knick-knack paddy whack, make this song your own!

(sung to the tune of "This Old Man")

This old man
Sings [/b/] songs.
He sings [/b/] songs all day long.
With a [b]ick-[b]ack [b]addy [b]ack,
Can you sing his song?
Join right in and sing along!

I've got some Torn Blakes for the Hungry Thing!

Corn Flakes

Feed Me!

Feed Me!

Phoneme manipulation is at its best in the humorous story *The Hungry Thing* by Jan Slepian and Ann Seidler. Read the story to your youngsters and then have them **respond to the literature** with this idea. Make a Hungry Thing, similar to the one shown, out of a paper grocery bag. Then encourage each child to bring a food label from home to feed this creature. During group time, direct the child to **replace a beginning, middle, or ending sound of his food's name with a new sound in order to make a nonsense word**. Then have the child hide his label as he announces what he brought. After students correctly guess the name of the food, have the child feed his label to the Hungry Thing. Be ready to repeat this activity several times because your youngsters are sure to get a kick out of making up silly words. Yum, yum!

Salad Days

Did you know salad is good for phoneme manipulation practice? It's true—try this tasty activity and see for yourself! In advance, purchase a variety of fresh vegetables whose names begin with consonants. Store the veggies in a large child-safe bowl and then gather a small group of students. Explain that you want to make a salad but first need help naming the ingredients. Then have each child, in turn, select a vegetable and say its name aloud. Encourage her to replace the first sound with another to give the veggie a new nonsense name. Give each child several turns to select and rename a vegetable; expect lots of silliness! At a later time, bring groups of students back to repeat the activity, this time manipulating the ending phoneme to make new words. Mmm, mettuce and womatoes. Please pass the dressing!

Old Mac's Adventures

Send Old MacDonald packing as your youngsters add sounds to existing ones to make new "words." As a group, decide where Old MacDonald should travel and then list some things he might see there. Modify one of the verses below to match the chosen destination; then substitute objects on your list for the ones shown. Change the "E-I-E-I-O!" line as needed by adding the initial sound of each object to the vowels. There's no need to finish the song each time; just keep naming different objects. Go, MacDonald, go!

Old MacDonald visits the [zoo].
E-I-E-I-O!
And at the [zoo] he sees a [zebra].
[Z]e-[Z]i-[Z]e-[Z]i-[Z]o!
And at the [zoo] he sees a [lion].
[L]e-[L]i-[L]e-[L]i-[L]o!

Old MacDonald visits the [park].
E-I-E-I-O!
And at the [park] he sees a [duck].
[D]e-[D]i-[D]e-[D]i-[D]o!
And at the [park] he sees a [bench].
[B]e-[B]i-[B]e-[B]i-[B]o!

Old MacDonald visits the [beach].
E-I-E-I-O!
And at the [beach] he sees a [shell].
[Sh]e-[Sh]i-[Sh]e-[Sh]i-[Sh]o!
And at the [beach] he sees a [jellyfish].
[J]e-[J]i-[J]e-[J]i-[J]o!

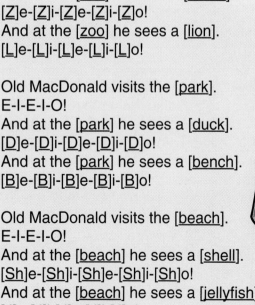

Prescription for Phoneme Manipulation

If you're hoping to ham it up with **letters and sounds in your next phoneme manipulation activity**, better make an appointment with the doctor—Dr. Seuss, that is! Read aloud *Green Eggs and Ham*. Afterward, call students' attention to the first sentence in the book by using magnetic letters to write "I am Sam" on a board. Read the sentence, pointing out each word. Then remove the *I* and read *am* and *Sam*. Ask your children what they hear as you say the words *am* and *Sam*. As they discuss that the two words rhyme, use the letters to show that *am* and *Sam* end with the same two letters, that *am* can become *Sam* if you add an *S,* and that *Sam* can become *am* if you remove the *S*. Focus on *am,* asking children to **think of other sounds that make words when followed by** *am.* Have volunteers say new *am* words and use magnetic letters to write them on the board. Provide support as necessary.

Continue to use *Green Eggs and Ham* for phoneme manipulation practice by reading further in the book. As you arrive at each of the following word pairs, stop to have students manipulate the phonemes as in the first activity: *house, mouse; box, fox; see, tree; rain, train; goat, boat.* Yes, we like them, Sam-I-am!

Cock-a-Doodle-Moo!

Rise and Shine!

Use Bernard Most's *Cock-a-Doodle-Moo!* to entice your children to play around with **phoneme manipulation and letter-sound correspondence skills**. Read the book; then revisit the pages where the rooster is trying to teach the cow the traditional wake-up call. Have children name each segment in the rooster's call. Use magnetic letters to spell *doo* on a board. Say, "Cock-a-doodle-doo," with the children several times, pointing to *doo* as you say it. Have children refer back to the book to see what the cow actually says. Say the cow's call with the children several times, emphasizing *moo*. Have a volunteer explain how the cow alters the last word segment, and then have him replace the *d* with an *m* to spell *moo*. Continue in this manner, having children **make substitutions for the first phoneme on the board**. At a later time, reread the book and repeat the activity, having children make substitutions for the *c* in *cock* or the *d* in *doodle*.

Three-Phoneme Picture Cards

Use with "Switcheroo!" on page 49.

LETTERS & SOUNDS

As your youngsters begin to advance beyond phonological awareness to make letter-sound connections, the activities that follow are sure to have them howling for more!

Studies have shown that incorporating letter-name and letter-sound instruction into phonological awareness activities increases success in reading development. However, it is important to note that once letters are used to represent sounds in phonemic manipulation tasks, the activity also becomes a *phonics* activity.

The activities in this section will help your students do the following:

1 understand the relation between letters and sounds

2 recognize letter symbols

3 match a sound with its letter(s)

4 match a letter with its name

5 match letters (or words) to objects that begin with specific sounds

Many opportunities to strengthen letter-sound connections occur naturally throughout the day. When planning activities, keep the following progression of skills in mind.

1. **Have an awareness of letter-sound connections.**
   Using letters as visual cues promotes the idea that symbols can represent sounds. Learning letter names and sounds can be done in conjunction with the first levels of phonological awareness, such as word awareness and rhyming.

2. **Use letters to represent sounds.**
   Once several letter names and sounds are learned, they can be used with other phonological activities, such as isolating phonemes, blending, and making words.

55

& Sounds   Letters & Sounds   Letters & Sounds   Letters & Sounds   Letters & Sounds   Letters & So...
...ds   Letters & Sounds   Letters & Sounds   Letters & Sounds   Letters & Sounds   Letter...

Bubble Gum, Bubble Gum

Put a twist on the traditional jump rope chant to help your youngsters **recognize letters and match them with their sounds**. To prepare, copy the gumball machine pattern on page 61 onto heavy paper and then cut it out. Collect a supply of colorful plastic counters to represent gumballs. Use a permanent marker to write a different letter of the alphabet on each one. Gather a small group of students around a table. Display the gumball machine with a collection of the lettered gumballs on it (vary the number to match the group's ability). Designate a child to be first; then lead the rest of the group in one of the versions of the chant below. Have the child pick a gumball from the machine and announce the letter's name or sound. Continue until each child has had a turn. "Chew-rific"!

This is **H!**

Bubble gum, bubble gum, in this game.
Which little gumball can you name?
(Student picks one and names the letter.)

Bubble gum, bubble gum, nice and round.
Pick a gumball and make its sound.
(Student picks one and makes the letter's sound.)

Bubble gum, bubble gum, a sight to see!
Can you find the [m] gumball for me?
(Student picks the piece to match the letter or sound you name.)

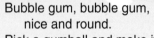

In go some w-w-w- worms!

As an extra ingredient, connect this idea with a piece of literature such as *Monster Stew* by Mitra Modarressi and *Ogres! Ogres! Ogres! A Feasting Frenzy From A to Z* by Nicholas Heller. Simply delightful!

Some Strange Alphabet Stew

Invite your youngsters to think like trolls, ogres, and monsters with an activity that stirs them to **match objects to their beginning letters and sounds**. You'll need a black plastic cauldron (or a pot), a wooden spoon, and a set of alphabet manipulatives. Divide the letters among the children in your group. Then explain that you're going to be making a special alphabet stew for your creature friends. Call out ingredients that need to be added. Pause after each one and encourage the child holding the letter that the ingredient starts with to drop it in the pot and stir. Continue adding ingredients until all of the letters are used. Or, for more of a challenge, have each child name his own ingredient to match the letter he is holding. Oh, can't you just taste this strange, but silly, stew? Eewwwww!

56

Letters & Sounds   Letters & Sounds   Letters & Sounds   Letters & Sounds   Letters & Sounds   Letters & Sou
& Sounds   Letters & Sounds   Letters & Sounds   Letters & Sounds   Letters & Sounds   Letters & Sounds

A Sticky Situation

This quick and easy activity encourages students to **match letters to objects that begin with specific sounds**. Simply grab a marker and a pad of self-sticking notes and you're ready! Give each child a sticky note with a different letter on it. Have him look around the room for something that starts with that letter and affix his note to it. Then provide an opportunity for each child to share what he found, and redirect if necessary. Have time for another round? Direct students to remove their notes and trade with a classmate. For lower ability levels, complete this activity in pairs. For higher ability levels, change to ending sounds instead of beginning sounds. It's a five-minute filler filled with fun!

Give Me A...

Here's something to cheer about—an idea that helps youngsters **match letters to sounds**! Dust off your pom-poms and head for the chalkboard. Choose an appropriate word for your students' ability levels. (If desired, use a seasonal or thematic vocabulary word to tie in with your current unit.) Then draw a box on the board for each sound in the word as shown. Now, let's cheer! Use the traditional "Give me a [b]!" chant, but call out the *sound* you're looking for. Have students reply by calling back the *letter* that makes the sound. Write the letter in the corresponding box. Fill in each of the boxes in this manner; then ask that ever so important question, "What have you got?" Help youngsters blend the sounds together to create the special word. Say it again! Hooray! As students get the hang of it, invite a volunteer to be the leader of his own cheer.

Listen and Do

Here's one idea that reinforces three skills: recognize letter symbols, match a sound with its letter, and match a letter with its name. Arrange a set of manipulative letters on a tabletop. Then, working with one small group of students at a time, designate a child to be first. Call out a direction such as those suggested in the list below, emphasizing the action that corresponds to the letter. Invite the child to use the letters to follow your directions. Vary the directions you use based on each group's abilities. Continue until each child has had a turn.

Sample Directions

- *Tap* the letter that says /t/.
- Put your *finger* on the letter that makes the /f/ sound.
- Pick up the letter that makes the /j/ sound and *jump* four times.
- Which letter makes the /n/ sound? Put that letter on your *nose.*
- Find the letter that says /p/. Now trace it with your *pinky.*
- Which letter makes the /d/ sound? Pick up that letter and *dance!*

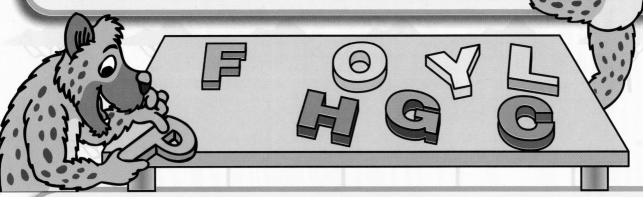

Mix 'n' Match

You'll be in awe of the progress made as you watch students work with letter-sound correspondence in this small-group activity! To prepare, gather a complete set of letter manipulatives for each child in the group. Instruct the child to find each of the following letters as you name them: *g, n, r, s, t, a, e, i.* Then, working with just those eight letters, prompt each child to see how many different words he can make by mixing and matching the letters. (If desired, use the script below or vary it according to your students' abilities.) Switch it, change it, rearrange it!

Mix 'n' Match Teacher Suggestions

- Find two letters to make the word *at.*
- Add one letter to make the word *sat.*
- Now, change one letter in the beginning to make the word *rat.*
- What letter can you add to the end of *rat* to make it more than one rat?
- Keep just the word *at.* What letter or sound could you put in the middle to make the word *ant?*
- Can you mix up those three letters to make the word *tan?*
- When you have the word *tan,* how could you change the ending sound to make the name of a game that you play outside where you say, "You're It!"? *(tag)*

58

Letters & Sounds Letters & Sounds Letters & Sounds Letters & Sounds Letters & Sounds Letters & Sounds Letters & Sou
& Sounds Letters & Sounds Letters & Sounds Letters & Sounds Letters & Sounds Letters & Sounds Letters & Sounds

How Does Your Garden Grow?

With letters, sounds, and words all in a row! This activity **connects letters with sounds** and brings them into full bloom. To prepare, cut the edges of ten paper plates, as shown, to resemble flowers. Use markers to decorate them and then write each of the following letters on a different flower: *a, t, b, c, f, h, m, p, r, s.* Have two students stand side by side holding the *a* and *t* flowers. Direct each child to make the sound of the letter on her flower; then encourage the rest of the class to blend the sounds to create *at.* Next, call out a word that can be made by adding one of the remaining letters to *-at.* Invite a volunteer to choose the correct flower and stand beside the *a* bloom to create the new word. Continue in this manner, giving other students opportunities to create new words.

Then store the flowers and a supply of the recording sheets on page 62 in your literacy center to cultivate more independent growth!

Word Builders

This playful word game will make your little learners flip! To make a flip booklet for each child, fold a sheet of 8½" x 11" paper in half lengthwise and staple it along the fold. Next, fold the paper into three sections and unfold; then cut along the top layer along the creases, stopping before the fold. Give a booklet to each child. Direct him to write the letters *b* and *p* on the first set of flaps (one letter per flap), *a* and *i* on the center set of flaps, and *n* and *t* on the last set of flaps. Use one of the booklets to demonstrate how to **build words by flipping through the individual letters, choosing three of them, and blending their sounds.** Allow students time to explore on their own; then make a list as the group works together to create as many words as possible. Can you make words? Yes, we can!

59

& Sounds   Letters & Sounds   Letters & Sounds   Letters & Sounds   Letters & Sounds   Letters & So
ds   Letters & Sounds   Letters & Sounds   Letters & Sounds   Letters & Sounds   Letters & Sounds   Letters

Doughnut Delights

Sweeten phonemic skills and letter-sound connections by using these doughnuts to **illustrate manipulating sounds within words**. To prepare, copy the patterns on page 63 onto construction paper to make ten doughnuts. (Or if desired, use the patterns to make craft-foam doughnuts.) Color and cut out the doughnuts. Then, with a permanent marker, label each doughnut, as shown, with one of the different letter pairs listed below. Store the doughnuts in an empty bakery box. Gather five six-inch paper dessert plates. In the center of each one, write a different vowel.

To complete the activity, arrange the plates on a tabletop. Have each child in a small group pick a doughnut from the box. Then direct each child, in turn, to place her treat on a plate so that it will make a word. As an extension, work with one doughnut at a time and switch plates to **change the medial sound**. Which doughnut will make the most words? Reward efforts with real doughnut holes, of course!

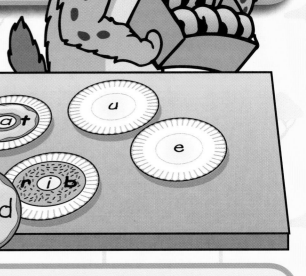

Carton Capers

If you have milk cartons, you have some great **objects to illustrate manipulating sounds within words**! Wash and dry six milk cartons from students' lunches. Use a permanent marker, tagboard, and craft glue to label each side of each carton with a different letter, putting consonants and vowels on different cartons. Arrange the containers so that they spell a consonant-vowel-consonant word, such as *cut, hop,* or *tan*. Next, have student volunteers (with you facilitating as necessary) **delete, add, or switch sounds in the word to make new words** by turning and/or moving the cartons. There are some "moo-velous" possibilities here for a great phonemic workout!

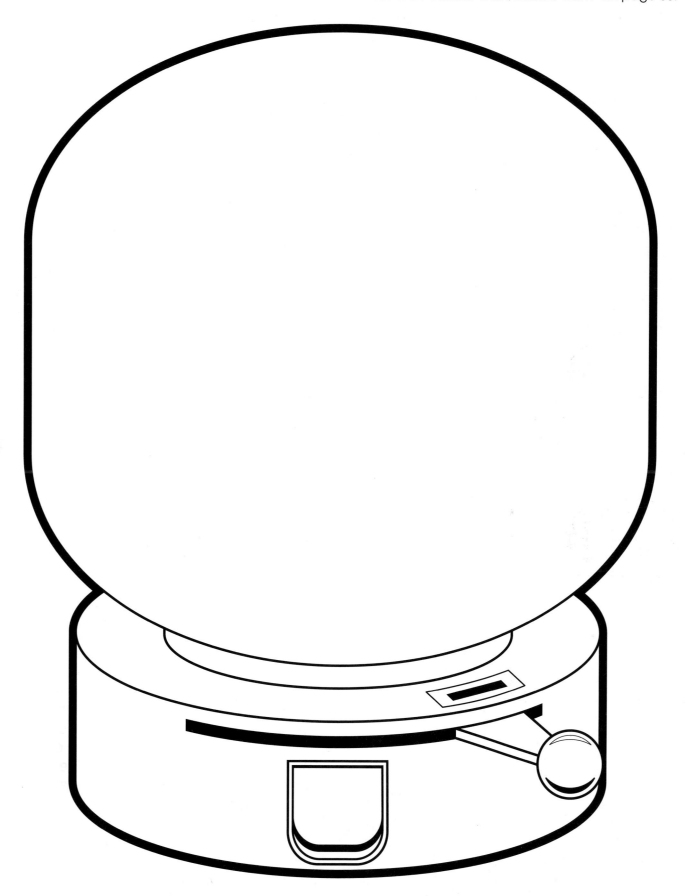

Use with "How Does Your Garden Grow?" on page 59.

Name________________________

Blooming With New Words!

Use these letters to make six words.

a t b c f h m p r s

Write.

1. ____________________

2. ____________________

3. ____________________

4. ____________________

5. ____________________

6. ____________________

Name________________________

Blooming With New Words!

Use these letters to make six words.

a t b c f h m p r s

Write.

1. ____________________

2. ____________________

3. ____________________

4. ____________________

5. ____________________

6. ____________________

©The Education Center, Inc.

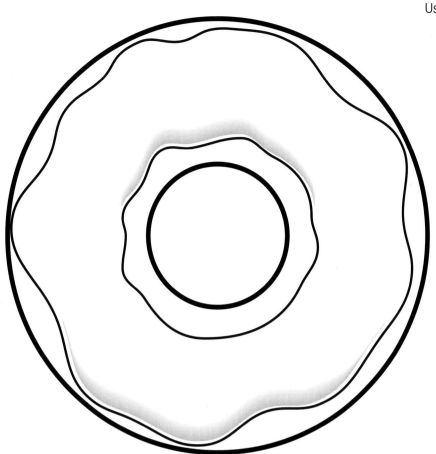

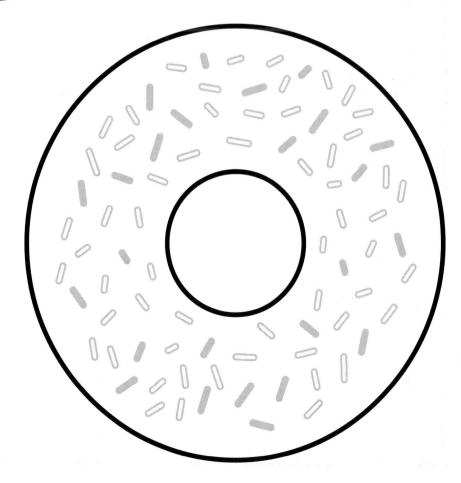

Name _____

Phonological Awareness Checklist

Skill	Date Assessed/+ or −			
The child demonstrates awareness of **rhymes** by				
recognizing rhymes (*Do* cat *and* hat *rhyme?*)				
discriminating between rhyming and nonrhyming words (*Which word does not belong*—fish, dish, fan, *or* wish?*)				
supplying rhyming words (*What word rhymes with* dog?*)				
The child demonstrates awareness of words or **word awareness** by				
putting words together to make sentences				
counting the number of words in a sentence				
The child demonstrates awareness of **phoneme matching** by				
matching beginning and ending sounds (b-b-bat, b-b-bowl, b-b-big—*what sound starts these words?*)				
grouping words with the same beginning, middle, or ending sound (*Can you put all the cards with pictures of items that start like* mouse *in a group?*				
identifying phonological oddities (Cat, hot, bug, nut—*which word does not have the same ending sound as the others?*)				
supplying sounds or words (*Name a word that starts with* /d/.)				
The child demonstrates awareness of **blending** by				
combining two words to make compound words (birth-day)				
combining syllables to make words (but-ter-fly)				
combining onsets and rimes to make words (sh-ip)				
combining individual phonemes to make words (s-t-o-p)				
The child demonstrates awareness of **segmenting** by				
separating sentences into words (*Clap for each word in this sentence: This is my car.*)				
separating compound words into smaller words (*Clap for each smaller word you hear in* pancake.*)				
separating words into syllables (*How many word parts are in the word* rabbit?*)				
separating words into onsets and rimes (*What is the first sound you hear in the word* shoe?*)				
separating syllables into sounds (*What three sounds do you hear in the word* cat?*)				
The child demonstrates awareness of **phoneme manipulation** by				
replacing the beginning, medial, or ending sound in a word to make a new word (Cat *becomes* can *by changing the ending sound.*)				
adding a sound to an existing word to make a new word (*/r/ with /am/ becomes* ram.*)				
using concrete objects, such as chips or letters, to illustrate manipulating sounds within words				
The child demonstrates awareness of **letters and sounds** by				
identifying letter symbols				
matching a sound with its letter(s)				
matching a letter with its name				
matching letters (or words) to objects that begin with specific sounds				

+ = aware
− = not yet aware